Lessons from a Cracked Pot

Lessons from a Cracked Pot

Yvette M. Blake

CONCLUSIO
HOUSE PUBLISHING

Printed in Canada
First Printing, 2015

ISBN 978-0-9949204-0-9

Published by:
Conclusio House Publishing
503-7700 Hurontario Street
Suite 209
Brampton, ON
L6Y 4M3

www.conclusiohouse.com

Unless otherwise stated, all scriptures from the Holy Bible are quoted from the New International Version (NIV)

This book is dedicated to my daughter, Nyashia James, and my grandmother, Hazel Williams.

Acknowledgements

Thanks be to You, God, for your wonderful transformation in my life. Words cannot adequately describe how grateful I am to you. Your love has captured my heart. Everything I am and hope to be is because of you. I adore you, Lord!

Special thanks to my grandmother, Hazel Williams, who raised me in the fear of God to become the woman I am today. I am eternally grateful for the sure foundation you laid for me. I love you, Mama.

To my mother, Janet Williams, and aunts, Rhona, Cecile, and Sharon Williams, who have been towers of strength in my life. I love and appreciate you for all you do.

To my wonderful daughter, Nyashia James, I treasure you for your insight, even at such a young age. You are the joy and love of my life.

My deepest appreciation to my pastors, Apostle Lovelace and Pastor Esther St. John of Progress Church, my spiritual parents who have guided and instructed me for many years to fulfill my purpose in God. You are my special inspiration. To my friends, Patricia McGregor Stewart and Jasmin Thompson Schloss, who encouraged me tremendously in my writing and assisted with proofreading, thank you for pushing me outside my comfort zone to answer the call of God. To my extended family, church family, and friends, who have been my faithful supporters and who have been there to strengthen my heart, thank you all for your unwavering support.

Table of Contents

Foreword

People can identify with the title *Lessons from a Cracked Pot* because of the feeling of being inadequate, or because life's struggles are beating them down and making them feel like a failure. Many give up their faith when confronted with challenges. Some believe we shouldn't go through hardships, but as iron goes through fire to be forged into a weapon, a tool, or a vessel, so it is that through hardship we are made into the man or woman God has already declared us to be. He has declared us to be conquerors.

"My troubles turned out all for the best - they forced me to learn from your textbook. Truth

from your mouth means more to me than striking it rich in a gold mine."[1]

I know that even a *cracked pot* has use; it can water others on their life's journey so that they will bloom. May God use your cracks to accomplish His purpose in your life and others.

Pastor Esther St. John
Progress Church of God

---

1   Psalm 119:71, MSG

Introduction

In our winter 2014 home cell group Bible study, I was reminded of the story of the cracked pot in one of our lessons. In the lesson, biblical characters were depicted as wonderful vessels for God's light to shine through. This reminder caused me to reflect on my own life, and I thought, *What a fitting metaphor!* You see, I am a cracked pot, not quite perfect. Thus began the blog "*Lessons from a cracked pot*", which I wrote as the Holy Spirit inspired my reflections. Through this process, God began to further heal my heart and show me that I didn't need to be "perfect", that He can use me for His glory and honour in spite of my failings, and even because of them.

In Isaiah 61:3 (NLT) God declares, "*To all who mourn in Israel, he will give a crown of beauty for ashes, a joyous blessing instead of mourning, festive praise instead of despair. In their righteousness, they will be like great oaks that the LORD has planted for his own glory.*" And I said, "*Yes, Lord, beauty instead of ashes!*" God is able to let His light shine through me. He is able to make beautiful that which was marred, broken, or charred.

I trust you will be blessed by reading these personal reflections of my heart. They speak of God's redemptive power and grace, and as you read you will see that your life can also be a wonderful vessel for God's light to shine through.

Yvette M. Blake

Not Quite Perfect

In a recent home cell group discussion, we were reminded of the story of the cracked pot, and it resonated with me.

The story is told of a water bearer in India who had two large pots, one hung on each end of a pole, which she carried across her neck. One of the pots had a crack in it. While the other pot was perfect, and always delivered a full portion of water at the end of the long walk from the stream to the master's house, the cracked pot arrived only half-full. For a full two years this went on daily, with the bearer delivering only one and a half pots full of water to her master's house. The perfect pot was proud of its accomplishments, perfect to the end for which it was made. But the poor cracked pot was ashamed of its own imperfection, and miserable that it was able to accomplish only half of what it had been made to do. After two years of what it perceived to be a bitter failure, it spoke to the water bearer one day by the stream: "I am ashamed of myself, and I want to apologize to you..." The water bearer said to the pot, "Did you notice that there were flowers only on your side of the path, but not on the other pot's side? That's because I have always known about your flaw, and I took advantage of it. I planted flower seeds on your side of the path, and every day while we walk back from the stream, you've watered them...

You see, a cracked pot represents someone who is not quite perfect. It represents someone who has been broken at some point in their life, someone who doesn't quite have it all together. Like me, many people are ashamed of their imperfections. We hold ourselves hostage to our past failures, mistakes, missteps, hurts, and sins. These things eventually become strongholds that the enemy uses to keep us trapped and unproductive in our lives. The question then becomes: Can God use a cracked pot? Can He forgive us, make us clean, and use us for His glory? The answer is an absolute yes! You see, when Nebuchadnezzar, king of Babylon, had taken the sacred vessels from the temple in Jerusalem, they became unclean and unholy, but they were not discarded.[1] They were returned by Cyrus, king of Persia, and rededicated for God's holy purpose after the rebuilding of the temple.[2] Like those vessels, we can become clean and holy again for God's use. Yes, God still uses cracked pots! I am a believer.

---

1   Daniel 5:1-4
2   Ezra 1:7

You Can't Move Forward While Looking in the Rear View Mirror

I was once asked the question, "Are you superior to God?" to which I answered with an emphatic "No." I was asked that question because, even though I had repented and God had forgiven me, I found it hard to forgive myself. I held myself to such high standards that I found it difficult to forgive myself for my failures. It wasn't until that question was posed to me that my healing began. God, in His divine providence, had forgiven me, so I had to forgive myself and allow His healing into my heart and soul. It was a healing process that took years.

As a child, I found that my parents didn't have to punish or discipline me, since I could do it all by myself. That's because I've always believed that events in my life derive primarily from my own actions, and thus I would tend to praise or blame myself or my abilities whenever something went right or wrong. I also found that I always learned from my mistakes and never wanted to repeat them, because they caused too much pain. You may be able to identify with having such an internal locus of control.

I have also learned that many years after your failure or sin has passed, some family members and friends, for whatever reason, may not want you to forget and move on. They were there to support you during your season of adversity, and you are grateful for that, but ultimately it was you who suffered the pain of your failures; you paid the price. And now, you have been forgiven and healed. You have learned your lessons. Yet, they fail to see this growth in you. They fail to trust you to make better decisions in your life. They feel it is their duty to constantly remind you of the past. Certainly, you have forgiven them seventy times seven as Christ commanded you to do, and have asked for God's wisdom in deciding who to allow to speak into your life on an ongoing basis. In other words, healthy boundaries must be put in place if you are going to be successful.

I am here to tell you that it's time to declare that the past is over, declare it dead in Jesus' name. *"Therefore, there is now no condemnation for those who are in Christ Jesus, because through Christ Jesus the law of the Spirit who gives life has set you free from the law of sin and death."*[1] You see, "your tomorrow will not be determined by what happened to you yesterday! Your tomorrow will be determined by what you believe about God. Too often we allow the hurts, failures, pains, and offenses in the rear view mirror to send us into the ditch to stay. We run off the road easily when we try to move forward while looking backward. You can get by with a backward glimpse to be reminded of where you have been. But do not stare and fixate on the road behind you."[2]

So leave the past behind and look ahead to the future with faith in God. As you trust Him, He will fill you with joy and peace and cause

---

1   Romans 8:1-2
2   From sermon by Apostle Lovelace St. John

you to overflow with hope by the power of the Holy Spirit.[3] Therefore, let us imitate the Apostle Paul and *"forgetting what is behind and straining toward what is ahead, [let us] press on toward the goal to win the prize for which God has called [us] heavenward in Christ Jesus."*[4]

---

3   Romans 15:13
4   Philippians 3:13-14

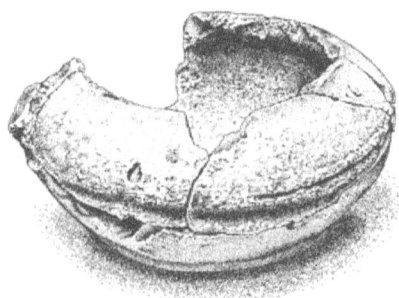

8

Find Hope in Broken Expectations

H ave you fallen short of your goals or disappointed yourself? Have you ever felt crushed when the things you expected in your life failed to materialize?

Expectations are things we anticipate will happen. Our expectations set us up for heartaches and disappointments, especially if what we are expecting does not come to pass. In other words, we anticipate results that are outside of our control or influence. It could be expectations about our relationship status, our finances, our spiritual life, or our emotions. We may even look at our age and stage in life and figure that we should be further ahead than we are, and we may become very disenchanted when things fail to manifest as we expected.

The Lord has been dealing with my heart about expectation versus hope. A year ago, I found myself in a rut, lost in unhappiness and despair. My unhappiness was due to the fact that what I expected for my life and the reality of what it was were out of sync. My inner critic was having a field day. You know that inner voice that condemns you and passes judgement? The one that tells you, "You're a loser," "You will never get what you desire," "No one will ever rejoice over your accomplishments." The one that says, "You don't deserve to be happy," or "Why be happy? Something bad is going to happen anyway." Being aware of this inner critic is the first step to victory, but don't be afraid to ask for help if needed. With help I learned to identify and show the critic the door and let God's voice in instead. The Word of God states, "*And be not conformed to this world: but be ye transformed by the renewing of your mind, that ye may prove what is that good, and acceptable, and perfect, will of God.*"[1] It's a struggle, but always remind yourself that God's voice calms, comforts, encourages, convicts, enlightens, stills, and reassures. Words of hopelessness, misery, or condemnation are not from God.[2]

In contrast to expectation, hope looks forward to something with desire and reasonable confidence. "*For in this hope we were saved. But hope that is seen is no hope at all. Who hopes for what they already have? But if we hope for what we do not yet have, we wait for it patiently.*"[3] Hope is connected to our belief, trust, and faith in God. Hope stretches our faith in God; it is attached to possibilities, not impossibilities. It is grounded in God through our prayers and steadfast faith. Hope anticipates a favourable outcome; it is a confident reassurance in God's track record. "*But those who hope in the LORD will renew their strength. They will soar on wings like eagles; they will run and not grow weary, they will walk and not be faint.*"[4]

1　　Romans 12:2
2　　Philippians 4:8
3　　Romans 8:24-25
4　　Isaiah 40:31

Hope is rooted in our faith that God has a plan for us. His plan is vast and comprehensive—*"For I know the plans I have for you," declares the LORD, "plans to prosper you and not to harm you, plans to give you hope and a future."*[5] God is our living hope and an anchor for our souls. *"Praise be to the God and Father of our Lord Jesus Christ! In his great mercy he has given us new birth into a living hope through the resurrection of Jesus Christ from the dead."*[6]

Hope does not disgrace, disappoint, or deceive. We can have hope in all situations *"because God has poured out his love into our hearts by the Holy Spirit, whom he has given us."*[7]

I choose to have hope in God. What about you?

---

5   Jeremiah 29:11

6   1 Peter 1:3

7   Romans 5:5

Ready And Waiting for True Love's Kiss

I read a blog post recently entitled "Being Single Isn't a Disease" by Jarrid Wilson. The essence of the article is that singleness should be embraced, that it is an opportunity to grow, learn, and experience life. The post encourages singles not to feel inferior or feel that being single is a flaw. It also reminds them that life can be fulfilling while single because singleness should not hold us back from accomplishing great things.

Though I certainly agree with the sentiments

expressed in the blog, it was written from the perspective of a married man. So, as a single lady, I wanted to give my honest feedback. Certainly being single is not a disease, but there are days when you do feel inferior to your married counterparts. You feel this way even though you are painfully aware that not all marriages are happy. Having experienced the pain of a marriage gone wrong, no one else knows this better than I do. So why feel inferior or that you are missing out? It is because ultimately we were created by God for relationship. So we long for that, we long to share deep friendship, companionship, intimacy, and our inner thoughts with another human being.

There are also days when loneliness can cover you like a cloak, and if you are not careful, you will get shrouded in the murky depths of despair. It is during these moments that you wonder if God is hearing your cry. Yes, you trust in His sovereignty and know you are where He wants you to be, you also know that He has good plans for you.[1] However, while veiled in the cloak of loneliness, it is hard to see ahead of you. I find that this loneliness is most evident during the

---

1   Jeremiah 29:11

weekend; on a Friday and Saturday night when you can't help but feel like there is nothing to look forward to, and the nights seem longer. So what do you do? You distract yourself, you shake off the cloak, you call your friends, you engage in meaningful activities that you enjoy, you get busy serving God and doing His will. Of course, some days this is easier said than done. Nonetheless, you get out there and experience life.

Another concern I would like to address is that of finding true love. Growing up, and even to this day, I find I thoroughly enjoy Disney movies; you know, *Beauty and the Beast, Princess and the Frog, Cinderella, Enchanted,* and the list goes on and on. Whenever I watch them, I am taken into an enchanted world, the one where you are enthralled when the main characters find "true love's kiss." I believe every little girl and grown woman, if they will admit it, longs for this.

Someone once told me that nothing is wrong with enjoying these movies, what we need to do is find our own true love and create our own real life enchanted story. Though there is some truth in this statement, I recently had to stop and analyze my attraction to these movies. Is it that I believe in fairytales? After careful examination,

I realized that it is not that I believe in fairytales, but that I believe in love, and I am fond of a happy ending. You see, all these movies have something in common, love always triumphs over evil. A happy ending, indeed. I know that in today's society the idea of true love has become tainted. What we consider to be true love is just infatuation, and most of us have been lied to so many times that we have been left disillusioned.

However, I still believe in the love described in the Scripture. I believe love conquers all. Love is patient, kind, and nurturing.[2] Love covers over all wrongs.[3] In a marriage covenant, husbands are instructed to love their wives as Christ loved the Church, and to love their wives as their own bodies.[4] Of course, wives ought to respect and submit to their husbands. Therefore, I encourage every single lady to choose wisely, to submit to true love and not to a counterfeit. Then, like the author of Songs of Solomon, you will be able to say, "*I found the one my heart loves.*"[5]

---

2   1 Corinthians 13: 4-13
3   1 Peter 4:8; Proverbs 10:12
4   Ephesians 5:22-33
5   Songs of Solomon 3:4

The Truth About Regrets

egrets, anyone? I've had a few. To regret is to feel sorrow or remorse for an act, fault, or disappointment. It is characterized as a sense of loss.[1] Regret is a negative conscious and emotional reaction to past acts and behaviours; it can be regret for an action or inaction. Regrets either burden us by decreasing present happiness or restricting future growth. They can also motivate

---

1   http://dictionary.reference.com/regret

us to move forward.[2] They burden us as we wish and wish we could have do-over's. We writhe in pain and wring our hands as we wish someway, somehow we could get the opportunity to redo or undo what we have done. To me, regret is similar to worry. They are both like a rocking chair—they give you something to do but get you nowhere, unless you use regret as a motivator.

Earlier in my life, after an action or inaction that caused some regret, I would ask many questions like, "Lord, why did this happen to me? Couldn't You have prevented this?" Or I would beat myself up with, "Why did I do that?" On and on the heart-wrenching would go. But I have learned that "Why me?" is not the question to ask. Instead, I have learned to ask, "What are the lessons that I need to learn from this?" "What is the Lord teaching me?" "Do I need to make amends?" "How can I apply the lessons learned?" From this perspective, I am better able to use regret as a motivator to propel me forward, and also ensure that I don't make the same mistakes twice.

---

2   https://en.wikipedia.org/wiki/Regret

So the question that begs to be asked is: Can we avoid having regrets in life? I believe the answer is no. There is always going to be remorse over an action we took or an action we didn't take. We live in an imperfect world, and we are all imperfect people. I believe the key is to recognize the regret quickly, take steps to correct the mess if necessary, learn our lessons, and move on. In other words, as children of God, another word for regret is *repentance*. Ask God for forgiveness, make amends, and forgive yourself. God is faithful and just to forgive us of our sins.[3] He also gives His grace, which is the empowerment we need to succeed in life.[4]

I have learned that though we cannot have do-over's, we can trust *"that God causes everything to work together for the good of those who love God and are called according to his purpose for them;"* in other words, in all things God works together with those who love him to bring about what is good.[5]

The Scripture also teaches us that we can be confident that He who began a good work in us will

---

3   1 John 1:9
4   2 Corinthians 12:9; Romans 5:17
5   Romans 8:28, NLT

carry it on to completion until the day of Christ Jesus.[6] Confidence gives us reassurance, security, and certainty. I can think of no better example of this than the Apostle Peter. In Matthew 26:69-75, Peter denied Christ three times. The Bible states that when he remembered the words Jesus had foretold, he went out and wept bitterly. What an example of deep regret but amazing repentance and transformation. Peter went on to proclaim the gospel of Jesus Christ with passion for the rest of his life.

Regrets, anyone?

---

6   Philippians 1:6

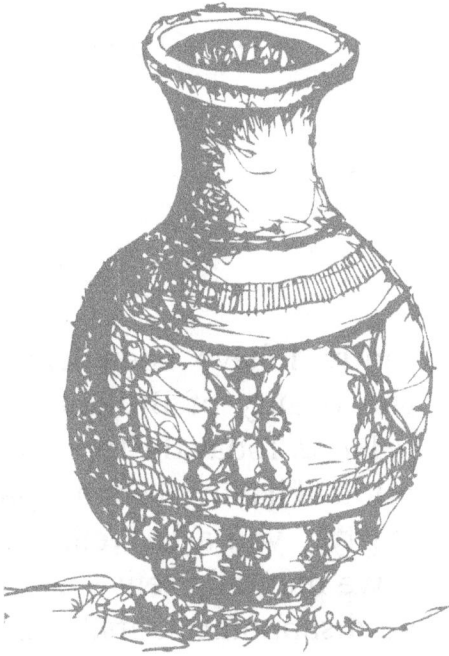

Beauty from Ashes

Recently, I have been learning about "The Beauty of Broken" on *Discover the Word*. Today the topic shifted to the notion of having a shame party. "What is a shame party?" you ask. Well, it's a solitary event where we mentally relive all our regrets, mistakes, and disappointments.[1] Oh, I have had many of those pity parties. But aren't parties supposed to be fun and festive, you know, good times? Unfortunately, shame or pity parties are

---

1 http://discovertheword.org/series/the-beauty-of-broken/

no fun at all. They are rather gloomy, joyless events in which we punish ourselves over and over again for past acts and behaviours. We tell ourselves we are bad, no good, and beat ourselves up for not getting it right.

Elisa Morgan of *Discover the Word* asked a very important question—"*What is wrong with the concept of having a shame party?*" She believes it's erroneous on several levels for the people of God. First, it makes us the centre of the universe, and we don't think about how we hurt other people. Second, it cuts us off from the love of God as we tell God who is worthy of His love and who isn't. In my mind, we become our own judge and jury, having predetermined that we are not worthy of God's love and mercy.

This discussion led me to reflect on the difference between shame and regret. In my recent entry, "The Truth About Regrets", I mentioned how regret can be a motivator to propel us forward as we learn the lessons that the experience taught us. Shame, on the other hand, is a painful emotion that leads to feelings of guilt, disgrace, and embarrassment.[2] Regret has a healthy component, while shame has an

---

2   Merriam-webster.com/dictionary/shame

unhealthy component. Regret is healthy because it can lead to repentance and forgiveness, while shame leads to judgment and un-forgiveness. In other words, shame leads to a dead end. Shame says that we are beyond fixing, there is no way out, or that we are capable of fixing ourselves (pride). Shame denies the fact that we are in need of a Saviour. What we need instead is regret, a path that leads to repentance, or what the Bible calls Godly sorrow—"*For the kind of sorrow God wants us to experience leads us away from sin and results in salvation. There's no regret for that kind of sorrow. But worldly sorrow [shame], which lacks repentance, results in spiritual death.*"[3] As we look to God with a repentant heart, He forgives us and purifies us.[4] A broken and a contrite heart He will not despise [scorn, look down on].[5] Afterwards, He makes us radiant with joy, and shame never covers our face.[6]

After some reflection, I thought, "How can what is broken be beautiful?" Think of all the things that have been broken throughout our lifetime. Don't we often throw away what is broken? But not God!

---

3   2 Corinthians 7:10, NLT

4   1 John 1:9

5   Psalm 51:17

6   Psalm 34:5

God says He makes beauty from ashes. Other words for ashes are *ruins, remains, leftovers, remnant,* and *residue.* Ashes are the result of fire, incineration, or combustion.[7] To me, it is the ultimate result of brokenness. I remember driving along in Zambia, Africa, and looking at the landscape after they burned the grass. From beneath the ashes, I could see new growth, that so fascinated me. Well, just like that grass that is burnt, but not without life, God is able to step down into the ruins and remnant of our lives, make something of beauty, *"and provide for those who grieve in Zion—to bestow on them a crown of beauty instead of ashes, the oil of joy instead of mourning, and a garment of praise instead of a spirit of despair. They will be called oaks of righteousness, a planting of the LORD for the display of his splendor."*[8]

What an amazing revelation!

---

7   Merriam-webster.com/dictionary/ashes
8   Isaiah 61:3

When You Lose Your Smile

I remember the time I lost, or should I say misplaced, my smile. It was shortly after getting married, then getting divorced. You see, my marriage only lasted ten months and left me broken and hurt. I totally believe in the institution of marriage and, for someone who is a perfectionist like myself, having something broken in my life was devastating. Prior to this happening, I was a relatively happy girl. As a matter of fact, I was very photogenic and had a beautiful smile. But after I lost my smile, I felt uncomfortable taking pictures; that happy smile just wouldn't come forth. I became un-photographable. Yes, my smile became lopsided and forced, my poses dull and unappealing. I didn't feel beautiful, and I certainly didn't want to be photographed. I lost my self-worth, my self-esteem, and sense of self. But thanks be to God, He restored me, and through the process of time my heart was healed and my smile slowly returned.

God is our healer. *"He was pierced for our transgressions, he was crushed for our iniquities; the punishment that brought us peace was on him, and by his wounds we are healed."*[1] Yes, He is the God that heals. This healing not only relates to our physical body, but also to the healing of our spirit and soul (our essence, core, and heart, which is the seat of our emotions) as well. He promises that "*weeping may stay for the night, but rejoicing comes in the morning.*"[2]

The process of my smile returning involved a healing of my mind and soul, and a transformation

---

1   Isaiah 53:5

2   Psalm 30:5

27

of my thinking.[3] I have come to realize that I must change my thinking in order to change my attitude and outlook on life. I recently heard that "*it's not what happens to you, it's what happens in you that make the difference.*"[4] You see, my thinking was keeping me from the joys of living. It told me that I had terrible stuff happen to me, that I deserved to walk around with an empty heart and a miserable outlook. As a result, my outward appearance reflected what was in my heart. But I have discovered that it is so much better to have a light heart, good thinking, and a positive attitude. That is why the Bible encourages us to think on what is lovely and pure.[5] Doing so takes way less energy, causes unexplainable peace, and has a positive impact on every area of our lives, including our relationship with God and others. Now I'm filled with joy. I can dance with my Father and let His light and glory reflect to those around me through my smile.

Selfie, anyone?

---

3   Romans 12:2

4   John C. Maxwell

5   Philippians 4:8-9

The Ten-Day Intentional Living Challenge

———— ༺❂༻ ————

For several months, I listened to Dr. Randy Carlson talk about intentional living, covering various topics on relationships, finances, faith, health, and work. I have also listened to John C. Maxwell and his teaching on our attitude being our choice. On July 21, 2014, the Holy Spirit inspired me to go on a ten-day intentional challenge to change my thinking and, by so doing, my attitude. You see, the Holy Spirit revealed to me that my thinking was especially negative. I desired a deeper walk with Him and greater purpose to my life. However, in order to accomplish what God had designed for my life, I had to change my thinking, intentionally.

The challenge: no negative thinking—over a period of ten days—about my life, my faith, my family members, my friends, my finances, my personal relationships, my career, and so on. Every time a negative thought came into my mind I would intentionally change it to a positive one by thinking on the Word of God in relation to that thought. What does the Word say about that thought or situation? I would think on what is lovely, pure, of good report, true, right, just, kind, worthy of reverence, honorable, and admirable.[1] I wanted the same attitude that was in Christ to be in me.

My negative thinking started when I immigrated to Canada over twenty years ago. Faced with adversity and new challenges, I began to withdraw into myself and started to think people were out to get me. These negative thoughts perpetuated and were later augmented by different painful life events, until they became

---

1   Philippians 4:8

a habit. These thoughts often led to anxiety, worry, fear, and unhappiness. I have come a long way in changing and improving my thinking, but have much growth left to do.

Over the ten days, I discovered that as I became intentional about focusing on my thinking, changing any negative thought into a positive one within a short time frame, it became easier and easier to think positively. I also found that the negative thoughts were not as intense or as influential in determining my attitude, thus I had a happier and more pleasant countenance. Little things that bothered me before didn't anymore. I discovered that we can't have a positive life with a negative mind. Positive thoughts cause our perspective and attitude towards life to change, and they make life so much easier to live. Our approach to situations also becomes clearer. I found that I learned to grow in prayer and actually trusted God for the outcomes.

I encourage you to take the intentional living challenge today.

Trusting God

After completing a ten-day intentional living challenge to transform my thought patterns, I began to reflect on what trusting God means. I thought I trusted Him but, after careful reflection, I realized that that was not the case. I read the Bible verses on trust, Proverbs 3:5-6 comes to mind—"*trust in the LORD with all your heart and lean not on your own understanding; in all your ways submit to him, and he will make your paths straight;*" I sang the songs—"I trust in you...I believe you're my healer...you hold my world in your hand." Yet I lived like none of this was true.

Synonyms for trust include faith, hope, belief, conviction, confidence, expectation, reliance, assurance, certainty, surety.[1] There are many things that I trust in life. I trust my car to take me from point A to point B safely, without the tires falling off or the brakes failing. I trust my bed to hold me up at night. I trust the roof of my home to not cave in on me. I trust the roads I drive on daily. I trust in so many manmade things, yet I often fail to trust my Heavenly Father for the outcomes of situations in my life.

So, what does it mean to trust God?

First I need to answer the question "What makes God trustworthy?" because I believe that the basic premise of trust is that the thing or person you are trusting in is worthy of that trust. In other words, is it credible? Can you be confident in or about it? Are you convinced that it will do what it says or be what it says it will be? In terms of a person, trust is usually based on

---

1 (Merriam-webster.com/dictionary/trust

their character or attributes. Character means "the mental and moral qualities distinctive to an individual or the aggregate of features and traits that form the individual nature of some person or thing."[2] God's distinctive nature is revealed all throughout the Scripture.

Theologians classify the attributes of God under two main categories—His infinite powers and His personality attributes.

His Infinite Powers

- **Aseity** – He exists in and of Himself; He exists eternally; He does not owe His being to any other thing (Exodus 3:4; Psalm 90:2; Acts 17:25; Colossian 1:15-17; John 1:1-5).

- **Oneness** – Refers to the unity of God and to Him being one (Deuteronomy 6:4; Mark 12:29; Ephesians 4:6).

- **Immutability** – He cannot change (Malachi 3:6; James 1:17; Hebrews 13:8).

---

2   www.dictionary.com/character

- **Transcendence** – He is vast, beyond all physical laws, outside space and time (Isaiah 57:15; Isaiah 55:8-9; Psalm 113:5-6; John 8:23).

- **Immanence** – His divine presence is near us, present and actively participating in the world (Jeremiah 23:23-24; Acts 17:27-28).

- **Impeccability** – He is unable to sin (Hebrews 6:18; Titus 1:2).

- **Incomprehensibility** – He is not able to be fully known (Isaiah 40:28).

- **Infinity** – He is eternal (Isaiah 40:28; 1 Kings 8:27; Psalm 102:12).

- **Omnipresence** – He is present everywhere in the fullness of His being (Psalm 139:7-10; Job 11:7-9; Psalm 90:1-2).

- **Omnipotent** – He is all powerful, El Shaddai (Matthew 19:26; Hebrews 1:3; Jeremiah 32:17; Romans 11:36).

- **Omniscience** – He is all knowing, nothing is outside the scope of His conception, understanding, or attention (Romans 16:27; Romans 11:33; Hebrews 4:13; Romans 2:16, Psalm 147:5).

- **Sovereignty** – He has divine control over everything that happens (Genesis 14:19; Exodus 18:11; Psalm 115:3; Matthew 10:29; Romans 9:15; Ephesians 1:11).

His Personality Attributes

- **Righteousness** – This refers to His holiness, justice and saving activity (Romans 1:17; Romans 9:14-33; Psalm 19:7-9; Psalm 145:17; Jeremiah 9:24).

- **Goodness** – He is the final standard of good, the source of goodness, kindness, love, mercy, and longsuffering (Romans 11:22; James 1:17).

- **Graciousness** – He is compassionate and gracious, forgiving, plenteous in mercy and grace (unearned and unmerited blessing)

(Exodus 34:5-6; 1 Peter 2:2-3; Psalm 145:17; Romans 3:24; Hebrews 4:16; Titus 3:5, 1 Peter 1:3).

- **Holiness** – He is separate from sin and incorruptible (totally pure) (Isaiah 6:3; Revelation 4:8; 1 Samuel 2:2; Psalm 99: 2-3)

- **Jealous** – An outflow of His covenant love for his people (Exodus 20: 5-6).

- **Love** – He is the source and genesis of agape, self-sacrificing and selfless (1 John 4: 8, 16; Romans 8:35-39).

- **Wrath** – He is against all evil (Exodus 15:7; Deuteronomy 9:19; Psalm 69:24; John 3:36).

- **Justice** – He is the ultimate judge over the lives and actions of men (Exodus 34:6-7; Genesis 18:25; Psalm 99:4; Romans 1:32).

All the above attributes and characteristics point to the trustworthiness of God. He is the source, the genesis of all that is good, lovely, and true. He is longsuffering and slow to anger.

2 Samuel 22:31 states that "*As for God, his way is perfect: The LORD's word is flawless; he shields all who take refuge in him.*" We can have confidence that He is credible. His goodness gives us security.[3] Nothing can separate us from His love.[4] What a wonderful reassurance. He died for us when we were His enemies, because He loved us, how much more shall He not freely and graciously give us all things? In Jeremiah 29:11, He reminds us that He has "*plans to prosper you and not to harm you, plans to give you hope and a future.*" His immutability means there is no change in His characteristics or plans and we can have faith in His sovereignty, knowing that no matter how chaotic our world becomes, He is still in control. He cares for us, and nothing is outside of His attention.[5]

So what does it mean to trust God? It means to rely on the integrity, strength, ability, and immutability of God's divine attributes and characteristics. It is believing that He is who He says He is and living our lives to reflect that belief. I believe, then, that our trust issues have nothing to do with God because He has revealed

3   Romans 8:28
4   Romans 8:38-39
5   Matthew 10:29

to us His divine nature throughout the Bible. I believe our lack of trust stems from our need to have autonomy over our own lives, as well as our desire to direct the course and outcomes of situations. When situations don't go as we planned, we blame God, even though we didn't seek His will and purpose in the first place. Trusting Him means that we leave the outcomes to Him regardless. It's relinquishing self-control and relying on Him fully. Trusting God is like taking a rollercoaster ride, once you get on and that ride starts all your control is gone. You must submit to the twists, turns, and bumps of that ride and believe that it will come to a safe end. How much more should be our trust in our loving Father? There is a blessing for us if we trust Him—*"Commit your way to the LORD; trust in him and he will do this: He will make your righteous reward shine like the dawn, your vindication like the noonday sun."*[6] *"But blessed is the one who trusts in the LORD, whose confidence is in him."*[7] He promised we will lack no good thing and that our strength will be renewed.[8] Amen!

---

6 Psalm 37:5-6

7 Jeremiah 17:7

8 Psalm 34:10; Isaiah 40:31

My Legacy

I grew up in the chilly, unflattering district of Coleyville, Manchester, Jamaica. My family was what you would consider poor, though, as a child, I never thought we were poor because I was treasured with love and my needs were always met. Our home was a small two-bedroom house that included a living room but no indoor bathroom or kitchen. A little anomy house, according to my grandmother. She would say, *"Dem say poorness a nuh crime, but is a hellava crime!"*

When I came on the scene, my grandmother had just lost her husband a few months prior and my mother was only a teenager. I grew up without a father, and I never knew my grandfather or great-grandfather. However, I knew my great-grandmother and grandmother.

My grandmother, Hazel Williams, who raised me, is a woman of faith. I also had the example of my great-grandmother, Eugenia Sergeant, who in due course passed away. My grandmother, whom I affectionately call 'Mama', not only instructed me in the way I ought to go, but she taught me about God, the Bible, and the great men and women who did exploits for Him. Moreover, she presented me to God daily in prayer. Mama demonstrated to me what it meant to serve God, to have faith in Him, and to trust in His provision. Her favourite saying is, "God good, Him good, Him good, you see!" as she often regaled me with stories of how God provided—from the small miracle of transportation when she needed to get to a destination, to the finances she needed to feed her family. As I previously stated, Mama lost her husband very early in life, and she was left with nine children to raise on her own. She was merely a farmer, but that didn't stop her from praising and serving God. I remember when she used to work in the fields, and I would leave home in search for her out in the bushes somewhere, and even though I didn't know exactly where to find her, I could always locate her from the sound of her singing. Yes, despite her hard circumstances, she would sing God's praises loudly, morning, noon, and night. Over and over again, demonstrating to the entire family what it means to serve God relentlessly.

You see, my legacy is not one of monetary gain, notoriety, or affluence. I have no great inheritance coming to me. It is not tangible or quantifiable. On the contrary, my legacy is one of unwavering prayer, faith, trust, and thanksgiving to an ever faithful, merciful, and gracious God. A God who has proven time after time that He is Jehovah! It is a foundation that stands sure.[1] This legacy I have received is enduring; it is what I have held onto when faced with adversities and challenges in my life. It is what has caused me to overcome, and not only survive but thrive. It is a prized possession, one that cannot be tarnished or stolen, for that, I am forever grateful. Through

---

1   2 Timothy 2:19

this bequest, I have discovered that God is a covenant-keeping God—"*He remembers His covenant forever, the promise He made, for a thousand generations.*"[2] Therefore, it is my belief that God will keep all the promises He made to my grandmother as she passes this legacy of faith on to her children, grandchildren, and great grandchildren.[3]

As I reflect on my childhood, God's faithfulness, and the legacy I have been given. I am challenged to leave a legacy, not only for my daughter, Nyashia, but for as many lives as possible with the time God has bestowed on me. I ask myself the following questions: *What am I doing with my life? What impact am I having on others? Am I here on Earth to just occupy space and use up resources?* The answer is no! My desire is to create a lasting legacy.

What about you?

---

2   1 Chronicles 16:15; Psalm 105:8
3   Deuteronomy 7:9

Forgiveness Is for You

Has someone hurt you, betrayed your trust, or rejected you? Maybe you have felt emotional pain so severely that sometimes you wish it were a physical wound that you could take painkillers or antibiotics to heal quickly. Maybe you have felt the pain of injustice and thought, *Why isn't the world taking notice?* You feel the world should stop and pay attention, if only for a second, and acknowledge that things are not right in your existence. Slowly, as you ponder the things done to you, the thorns of resentment formulate and take hold. You've known about forgiveness all your life, and before this hurt you were always forgiving. But this hurt is deeper than you have ever known, and you feel injured beyond measure.

You think, *I can't forgive. If I forgive, I'll forget the pain and hurt, and I want to make sure I remember this, remember how this person made me feel, remember what he/she did to me.* You believe the person is out there waiting for your forgiveness, and you think, *I have to hold onto the pain and anger, because by not forgiving I'm punishing this person.* But oh, what a lie that is. The person may have moved on or may not even be aware of the depth of the pain they have caused. They may be quite happy, while you are writhing in anguish and anger.

I experienced this in my own life, and I believed that by not forgiving I was punishing the person, when in actuality I was punishing myself. My heart was the one that was bitter, and my heart was the one that was hurting and sorrowful beyond measure. Who knows how the person that caused the hurt felt? Sometimes you feel that you're only going to forgive if the person asks to be forgiven, or if they say they're sorry. However, they may never ask or show remorse, or they may not be accessible to you anymore.

So what is forgiveness? It is "the intentional and voluntary process by which a victim undergoes a change in feelings and attitude regarding an offense, let's go of negative emotions such as vengefulness, with an increased ability to wish the offender well."[1]

Yes, forgiveness is a change in perspective on your part, and a change in the way you view the offense done to you. The Bible certainly has plenty to say about forgiveness; the basic premise, however, is *"forgive and it shall be forgiven you."*[2] In other words, if we forgive each other, then our Heavenly Father will also forgive us.[3] In the Bible, there is no basis for when we ought to forgive or how many times to forgive;[4] therefore, our forgiveness should not be contingent on what the person who did the

---

1   https://en.wikipedia.org/wiki/Forgiveness

2   Luke 6:37

3   Matthew 6:14-15

4   Matthew 18:21-22

misdeed against us does. Meaning, if they don't repent, we should still forgive. *"Bear with each other and forgive one another if any of you has a grievance against someone. Forgive as the Lord forgave you."*[5]

We are to forgive, period. Is this easy to do? The answer is no, but I believe once we forget the lies about trying to penalize or waiting to be asked for forgiveness, we will become conscious of the fact that forgiveness is for us. "Why is it for us?" you make ask. It is for us to release the anger, the bitterness, and the hurt from our hearts. Forgiveness allows us to let go of negative emotions and causes the healthy emotions of love, kindness, and empathy to flow in our hearts. Forgiveness releases us from the prison of pain. The ultimate test of forgiveness is when you can recall the misdeed done to you, and it causes you no pain, and you feel no ill-will against the perpetrator. When you forgive, you are no longer a prisoner, you are free!

---

5   Colossians 3:13

49

Order Up

Have you ever been in a restaurant and heard the cook yell to the waiter or waitress, "Order Up!"? This means the meal is ready to be served to the customer who ordered it. I was reflecting on life recently and some of the lessons it has taught me, and this phrase came back to me. "Order up" is what life says to us sometimes. It may be the death of a loved one, a terrible medical diagnosis, the loss of a job, or the pain of a broken relationship. Whatever the end result, when life says, "Order up," it rarely notifies you first or gives you a rationale. Many have grappled with this concept of life. Is it fate? The gods? The fact is none of the brokenness and pain that is in our world would be occurring if our fore-parents, Adam and Eve, didn't sin in the Garden of Eden. With their one act of disobedience, suffering entered our once beautiful world. But our Heavenly Father, in His sovereignty, made a way, and we can be sure that His grace is sufficient.

When life says, "Order up," it is your turn; and unlike a restaurant, you can't erase your name. You can't say, "I didn't order this. I don't want it. Take it back." Our choices are simple—deal with it, fight it, let it win, or change our attitude and perspective about it and overcome it. In other words, we cannot get out of the order. Oh, how we often want to escape and run away. We ask ourselves, *Why did life call my name?* However, our loving Heavenly Father has promised to give us the strength to endure whatever may come our way. He said to the apostle Paul in 2 Corinthians 12:9, "*My grace is sufficient for you, for my power is made perfect in weakness.*"   Yes, indeed, all through Scripture we have seen God be there for

His people. In Psalm 46:1, the psalmist declared, *"He is our refuge and strength, an ever present help in trouble."* He is not only our strength, but He is also our God of all comfort. *"Praise be to the God and Father of our Lord Jesus Christ, the Father of compassion and the God of all comfort, who comforts us in all our troubles, so that we can comfort those in any trouble with the comfort we ourselves receive from God."*[1]

Our aptitude to survive life's challenges will be predicated on knowing that they come not to destroy us but to make us stronger. The 'order' we receive in life will threaten and even rock the stability of our world. We may feel off kilter for a long time, even lopsided. We must, however, know that through God we are a match for whatever life may throw our way. We can have full confidence in His power to sustain and keep us.[2] Therefore, we must endure and persevere through our difficulties, for though we may be mystified, confounded, baffled, and bewildered, we are not dejected, desolate, or hopeless. *"For everything that was written in the past was written to teach us, so that through the endurance*

---

1   2 Corinthians 1:3-4
2   2 Corinthians 4:8-9

taught in the Scriptures and the encouragement they provide we might have hope."[3] We can endure and persevere through life's "order up" because we trust in God. Peter declares that He is our living hope,[4] which gives us confidence and self-assurance that as we overcome one challenge it gives us hope to face the next.

Romans 5:3-5 says, "*And not only this, but we also exult in our tribulations, knowing that tribulation brings about perseverance; and perseverance, proven character; and proven character, hope; and hope does not disappoint, because the love of God has been poured out within our hearts through the Holy Spirit who was given to us.*"

There is hope for the living!

---

3   Romans 15:4
4   1 Peter 1:3

Bad Things Do Happen
to Good People

Growing up, I was always adored by both my family and the people around me. People would say, "You're so cute," "You're adorable," "You're sweet." My grandmother would tell me that my face was cute like a button and my nose like a thimble. Back then, I knew my grandmother, whom I called Mama, as my mother, and my mother as my aunt. My aunts were especially kind to me and they would take me everywhere they were going. My Aunt Cis, in particular, would always tell people that I was her daughter. As I grew into a teenager, I learned that Mama was actually my grandmother, and I struggled with the notion that I had many caregivers, but I didn't really belong to anyone. Later in life, however, I came to appreciate all the love and care I received, and now I believe I was very blessed to have many wonderful mothers who mothered me.

It is with this backdrop in mind that somehow, unconsciously, I grew up believing the myth that because I am a sweet, beautiful, kind person that bad things would not happen to me, or that the world would be kind. *Why would anyone want to hurt me when I try my best not to hurt anyone?* I thought. Why do bad things happen to good people, period?

Maybe you can identify with this sentiment. You may wonder what you did to deserve your situation. Or you may think that God is unjust and is out to get you. However, God is just, "*He causes his sun to rise on the evil and the good, and sends rain on the righteous and the unrighteous.*"[1] We live in a fallen world, and it doesn't matter

---

1   Matthew 5:45

who you are, corrupt or unfortunate circumstances will find you. Nevertheless, I have learned to "*give thanks in all circumstances; for this is God's will for [me] in Christ Jesus.*"[2] I also have full confidence in my Creator and trust His Word when He tells me in Romans 8:28 that in all things He works for my good because he loves me.

Therefore, despite the bad, I still do good to all I come in contact with. Besides, I'm still cute!

---

2   1 Thessalonians 5:18

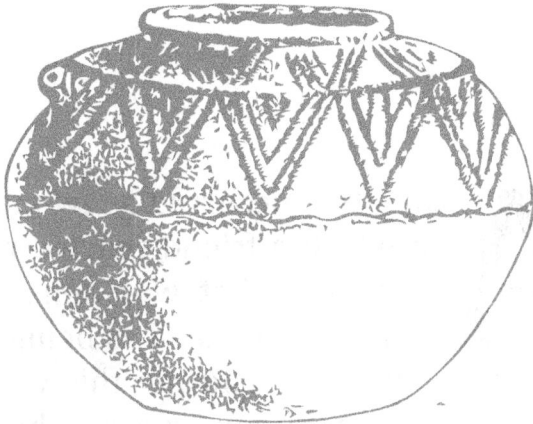

A Matter of Perspective

A situation occurred a few months ago in which a friend reacted negatively to a deed that was done for her. I regarded the deed as being kind and thoughtful, but my friend felt this was not the case and that the person who did the deed did not really take the time to know what she liked. As I watched my friend's reaction, I thought to myself, *I would love if someone did that for me or even had it in mind.* I came to the profound realization that life is a matter of perspective.

What is perspective? Perspective is our outlook, the way we view things, our attitude towards or the way we regard or interpret something.[1]

We have all heard the old adage, "Is the glass half-full or half-empty?" Half-full represents a view of life that is optimistic, while half-empty represents a view that is pessimistic. Well, I also recently heard that some people say the glass isn't even there, which in my mind represents a view that says there is no opportunity for improvement, or life's situation is hopeless.

Similarly, I was in a social setting recently, and as I listened to someone speak about their life, I began to view my life as half-empty. The person spoke of working in different countries and being able to travel to many places for vacation. Places I would like to go. Their life sounded so much more exotic than mine. So I allowed my thoughts to run away with me, and I began to ask questions like, *Why is my life so deprived and boring? How come I don't get the same opportunities? Is it because of my race or where I was born or the family I was born into?* However, as I began to reflect, I remembered that when

_____
1   https://www.google.ca/#q=perspective

I had visited Zambia a few years ago I was considered a multimillionaire with the limited Canadian dollars I had taken with me. This caused a shift in my perspective, and I thought to myself, *I am in a wealthy place.* A wealthy place not just financially, but a wealthy place physically, emotionally, mentally, and spiritually.

Yes, my glass is undeniably half-full, even to the brink of overflowing!

Viewing the glass half-full or half-empty is what philosophers refer to as the difference between idealism and realism. Idealism is picturing things as you imagine they would or should be, while realism is viewing things as they are. Idealism gives us direction and vision, while realism gives us practicality and traction. Both have downsides—realism can cost us our dreams while idealism can consume us with the futile search for the perfect life or happiness. What we need is balance. Even though the Bible does not use the word perspective, God's Word certainly has a lot to say about how we ought to view and live our lives in a balanced way. The Bible portrays a harsh realism. It tells us that in this life we will have many trials and testin

Jesus said in John 16:33[2], *"I have told you these things, so that in me you may have peace. In this world you will have trouble. But take heart! I have overcome the world."* This realism is recorded many other places in Scripture. In James 1:2-4, we are told to *"consider it pure joy, my brothers and sisters, whenever you face trials of many kinds, because you know that the testing of your faith produces perseverance. Let perseverance finish its work so that you may be mature and complete, not lacking anything."* The truth is that although the Bible gives us a practical view of life, it doesn't leave us there. It also provides the ideals for living. It tells us to *"give thanks in all circumstances; for this is God's will for you in Christ Jesus."* Romans 8:28 reminds us that in all things God works for our good. The psalmist reminds us, in various chapters, to bless the Lord at all times and to forget not the Lord's benefits, even in the midst of all our difficulties.[3]

Every day we have to choose whether we are going to be a half-full or half-empty person. This depends on how we view our present situation,

---

2   1 Thessalonians 5:18

3   Psalm 34; 103

our inadequacies, and our past failures. Are we going to compare ourselves with others? Or are we going to recognize what we have and be grateful? The word optimism is derived from the Latin word *optima* meaning the best possible outcome or belief that good will prevail. Psychologists have found that seeing the glass half-full not only makes us happier, it also makes us healthier and wealthier.[4] From a Biblical perspective, this equates to a balanced life, a life filled with joy, peace, and hope.

It's up to you; your view and attitude will determine your trajectory.

---

4   Warrell, Margie, 2012.

Loving Completely: The Response of Love

T he word love is increasingly being used more loosely in our society. Artists shout to screaming fans, "I love you!" and fans scream all the more loudly the same words back. While nothing is inherently wrong with this notion of love, the fact is the world has become more cynical of love and what it really means to love. This is because love is linked to conditions and false sentimentalities. As humans, we ought to have a rudimentary love and respect for our fellow human beings.

This basic love and respect is the basis of our humanity; it is what will prevent all the possible atrocities of mankind. It is why the majority of people in our society are not murderers, thieves, or rapists. Remove love and the result would be hate and the mass destruction of lives.

However, the premise of love is that there is a commitment, not just a sentimental feel-good notion. The best example of real love is found in our Creator God. *"But God demonstrates his own love for us in this: While we were still sinners, Christ died for us."*[1] Yes, when we were His enemies He died for us to reconcile us back to Himself. Jesus declared in John 15:13, *"Greater love has no one than this: to lay down one's life for one's friends."* In other words, the highest instance of love among humankind is giving one's life for another. So what then is love? How can it be encapsulated? Love in its essence is sacrificial, love is unconditional, love is patient, love is forgiving, love is faithful, love is kind, love is compassionate and tender-hearted, and love is selfless and boundless. It is doing good to

---

1   Romans 15:8

others, even when it is not done for us. It is captured by what we call the golden rule—do to others what you would have done to you.[2] It is doing things to encourage, affirm, build up, support, comfort, bless, and help someone. It is seeking their good, rooting for their success, hurting when they hurt, and being elated at their triumphs. Love is a best friend that pursues your greatest interest, that will say, "I am for you. I got you." Love is a companion that will go through the ups and downs of life with you, that will cherish you, that sees your flaws and loves you anyway.

This is the agape love from which all other loves stem, whether it be love between a parent and child, love between friends, or romantic love between a man and a woman. God, in loving us unconditionally, has captured our hearts and has won our affection.[3] Therefore, he has instructed us to *"Love the Lord your God with all your heart and with all your soul and with all your strength and with all your mind'; and, 'Love your neighbor*

---

2   Matthew 7:12
3   1 John 4:19

as yourself.'"[4] Several years ago, I came to the realization that if we were not capable of giving this kind of love, the Lord would not have commanded us to love like this. For it is indeed a command, not an option. This has caused me to disregard the cynics who say I love too much. How can I love too much when my Father has commanded me to first love Him then love my fellowman? In Philippians 1:9-11, the Apostle Paul prayed that *"Your love will flourish and that you will not only love much but well. Learn to love appropriately. You need to use your head and test your feelings so that your love is sincere and intelligent, not sentimental gush.*

Live a lover's life, circumspect and exemplary, a life Jesus will be proud of: bountiful in fruits from the soul, making Jesus Christ attractive to all, getting everyone involved in the glory and praise of God" (MSG). He was saying that God wants us to not only love more but to also love well as we grow in knowledge and understanding. This is done by cultivating a heart that is free from cynicism, condemnation, and callousness; essentially, loving others, no matter how much

---

4   Luke 10:27; Deuteronomy 6:5

we know about them. Love is therefore a process, a journey, not a destination. It is an expedition to achieve the highest form of love—the agape love.

1 Corinthians 13:4-8 says, *"Love is patient, love is kind. It does not envy, it does not boast, it is not proud. It does not dishonor others, it is not self-seeking, it is not easily angered, it keeps no record of wrongs. Love does not delight in evil but rejoices with the truth. It always protects, always trusts, always hopes, always perseveres. Love never fails. But where there are prophecies, they will cease; where there are tongues, they will be stilled; where there is knowledge, it will pass away."*

Love much. Love well!

Fretting: What's Wrong with That?

"Do not fret—it only causes harm!"

These words from Psalm 37:8 jumped out at me from a recent devotional I read. I had read this Psalm many times. It is the Psalm that talks about delighting yourself in the Lord and Him giving you the desires of your heart, or committing your way to the Lord and Him bringing forth your righteousness as the light of dawn and your justice as the noonday sun. Yet, on this day, these words caused me to pause and take another look.

Fretting means to be vexed or troubled; to be

worn or eaten away; to gnaw with the teeth like a rodent. Its synonyms include anxiety, care, worry, and distress.[1] Fretting is one of God's great don'ts. Yet, I must admit, this is an area in my life that I struggle with. It is like I was programmed to fret, though I know fretting causes harm, not only spiritually, but also mentally and physically. Whenever I worry and fret, I can't sleep, then I become weary and overwhelmed, and like a deer caught in the headlights, my ability to function mentally diminishes. Not to mention the effects on my emotional and physical health. It would appear, then, that fretting produces nothing good other than giving me something to do.

It is easy to say, "Do not fret." We have heard it said many times over, but it is something quite different to have a temperament where you find yourself unable to fret. The opposite of fretting is finding rest, assurance, ease and peace. So how do we not fret in all the difficulties and challenges of life? How about not fretting, simply because Jesus said so? Jesus told his disciples not to worry about tomorrow and not to worry about life.

---

1   www.thefreedictionary.com/fretting

"Therefore I tell you, do not worry about your life, what you will eat or drink; or about your body, what you will wear. Is not life more than food, and the body more than clothes?"[2] We fret because we feel God can't handle our concerns, so foolishly we take them on and believe that by fretting we will somehow solve our issues.

To not fret means we put our trust and faith in God Himself, resting in him despite the external circumstances all around us. I have proven in my own life that when I follow the principles found in Philippians 4:6-7, I find such indescribable peace, rest, and restoration for my soul, despite the unfavourable circumstances raging all around me. Yes, the peace of God will guard our minds, acting as an umpire in a boxing ring, arbitrating between the contending forces of anxiety and worry to maintain our mind and soul in rest. This peace comes by bringing our worries and concerns before God through prayer, petitions, and praise, and leaving them with Him. Certainly, abiding in God's rest and peace is an intentional choice we must make daily, even several times throughout the day. Jesus invites us to cast our cares on Him because He cares for

---

2   Matthew 6:25, 34

us, and in return we will find rest.[3] This requires action on our part, a purposeful conscious decision to throw our burdens on the One who is able to carry it for us. It's a putting down and a taking up—putting down cares, anxieties, and frets, and taking up rest, peace, and joy. What a beautiful trade off to fretting!

---

3   Matthew 11:28-29; 1 Peter 5:7

Resources

- "Dictionary.com - The World's Favorite Online English Dictionary!" www.dictionary.com

- "Dictionary, Encyclopedia and Thesaurus." *The Free Dictionary*. Farlex. www.thefreedictionary. com.

- "Difference Between Idealism and Realism | Difference Between | Idealism vs Realism." www.differencebetween.net

- Family Life Radio by Intentional Living Center. Used with permission. All rights reserved. www.theintentionallife.com

- *Forbes.* Forbes Magazine. www.forbes.com.

- Google. www.google.ca

- Holy Bible, New International Version (NIV) 2011 by Biblica Inc. www.biblegateway.com

- Holy Bible, New Living Translation (NLT) 2013 by Tyndale House Foundation. www.biblegateway.com

- Holy Bible, The Message (MSG) 2002 by Eugene H. Peterson. www.biblegateway.com

- Merriam-webster Dictionary www.Merriam-webster.com/dictionary

- "*My Tomorrow is Better than My Yesterday.*" Apostle Lovelace St. John. Progress Church, Toronto, ON. Dec. 29, 2012.

- "Study Resources: The Attributes of God." *Blue Letter Bible.* www.blueletterbible.org.

- *"The Beauty of Broken."* Discover The Word®, © 2014 by RBC Ministries.
  Used with permission. All rights reserved. www.discovertheword.org

- *"Your Attitude: Key to Success: Maintaining a positive attitude can contribute to success."* Dr. John C. Maxwell. Used with permission. All rights reserved.

- *Wikipedia.* Wikimedia Foundation. www.wikipedia.org.

About the Author

Yvette M. Blake is the mother of an amazing thirteen-year-old daughter, whose life is a daily reminder of the grace and incredible beauty of God. She believes being a mother is her highest calling and her greatest responsibility. Yvette holds a Bachelor of Science Degree in Nursing, a Master of Health Studies Degree, and an associate degree in Christian Studies from the Sure Foundation Theological institute. She currently lives with her daughter in Ajax, Ontario.

Lessons from a Cracked Pot is her first published book.

www.ingramcontent.com/pod-product-compliance
Lightning Source LLC
Chambersburg PA
CBHW072045040426
42447CB00012BB/3022